Volume Seven
-Intermediate

Accent on
GILLOCK

by William Gillock

CONTENTS

ISBN 978-0-87718-082-1

Exclusively Distributed By

HAL•LEONARD®

© 1995 by The Willis Music Co.
International Copyright Secured   All Rights Reserved

Visit Hal Leonard Online at
www.halleonard.com

Contact us:
Hal Leonard
7777 West Bluemound Road
Milwaukee, WI 53213
Email: info@halleonard.com

In Europe, contact:
Hal Leonard Europe Limited
42 Wigmore Street
Marylebone, London, W1U 2RN
Email: info@halleonardeurope.com

In Australia, contact:
Hal Leonard Australia Pty. Ltd.
4 Lentara Court
Cheltenham, Victoria, 3192 Australia
Email: info@halleonard.com.au

To my friend, Nina M. Stackpole

Castanets

William Gillock

Steadily, in slow motion

* Shading and touches *simile* throughout.

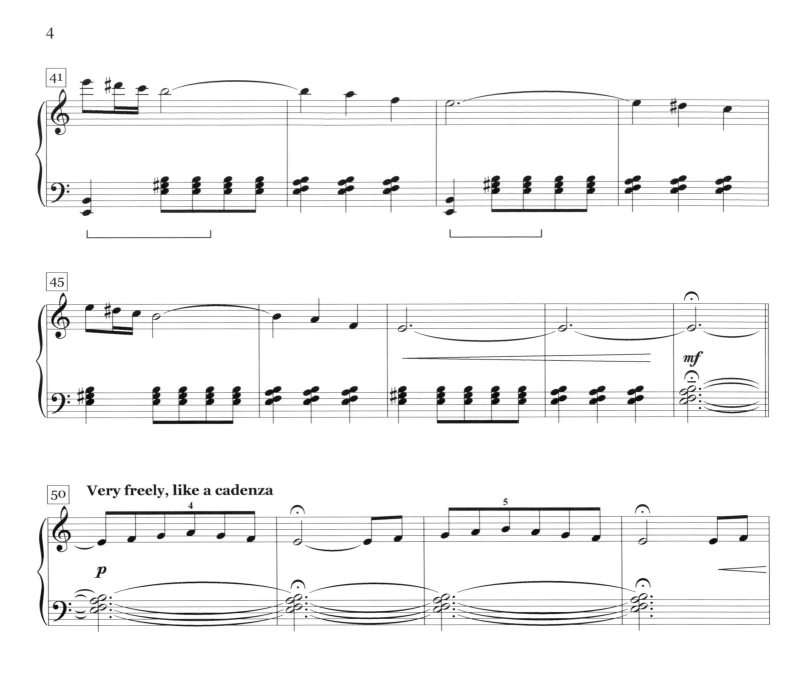

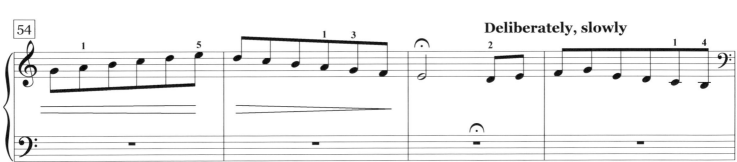

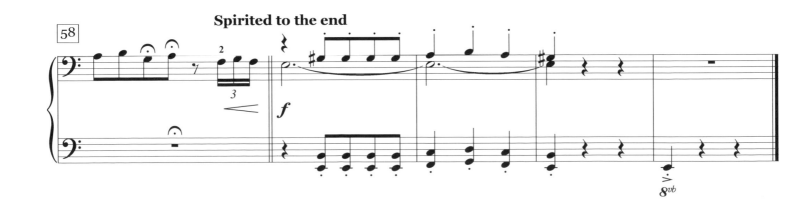

Ariel
(A Forest Sprite)

William Gillock

Commissioned by
The Piano Teachers' League of Hattiesburg, Mississippi

Sevilla

William Gillock

A vibrant Spanish dance

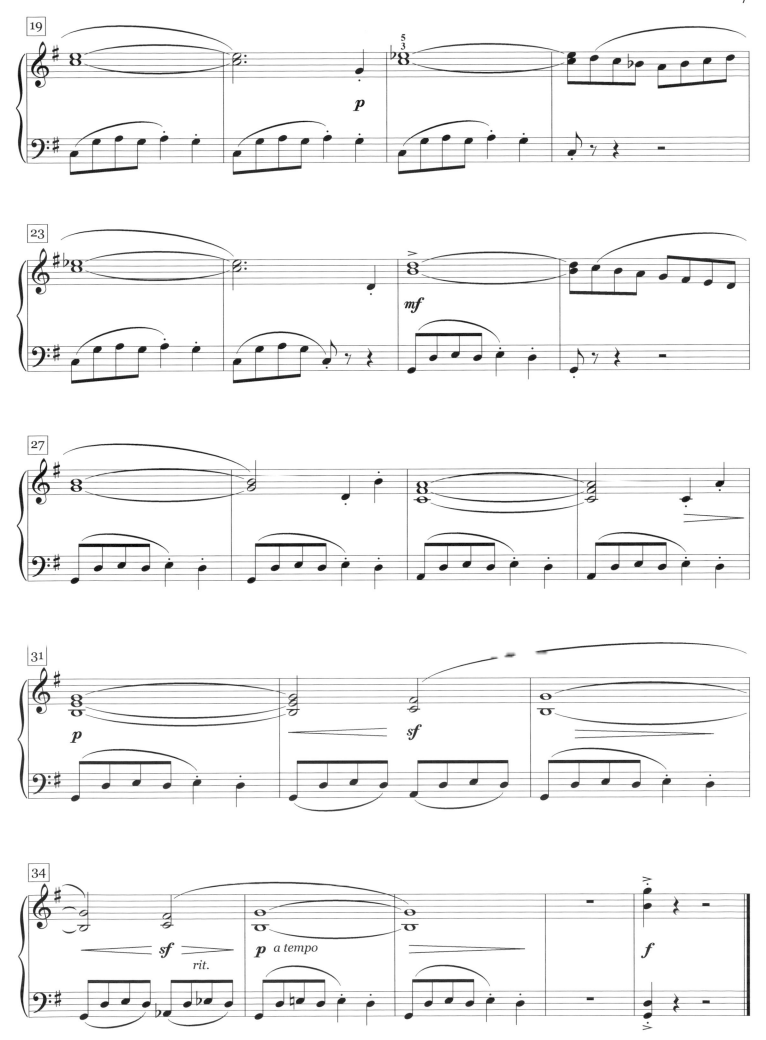

Blue Mood

William Gillock

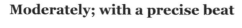

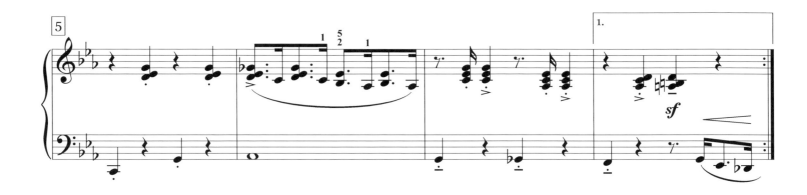

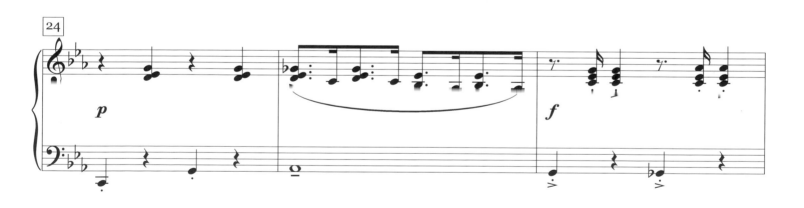

In Old Vienna

William Gillock

Tempo di valse Viennese

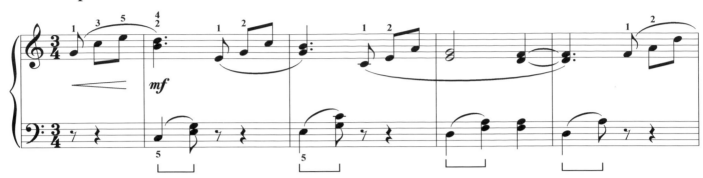

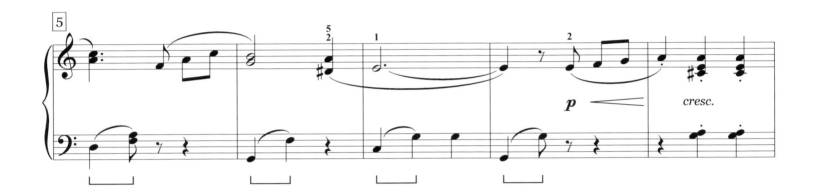

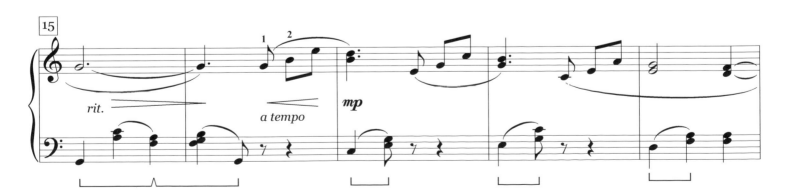

Fondly dedicated to the 80th anniversary of
The New Orleans Music Teachers Association

Dusk on the Bayou

William Gillock

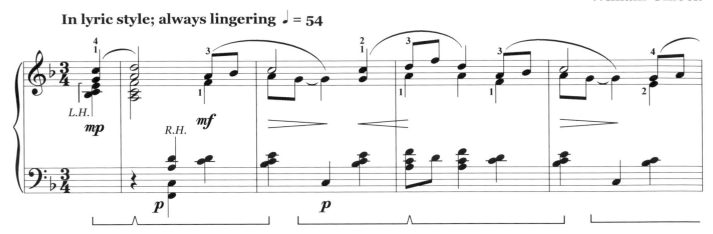